Shift The World

Apostle Mark A. Haywood

Sacred College Press
Fort Wayne, Indiana

Shift The World By Mark A. Haywood

ISBN 978-1-387-31144-6

First edition 2017

Dedication

This book is dedicated firstly to my King, the God of Abraham, Isaac, and Jacob, our Father, YHWH, and His Son, Jesus Christ (Yeshua HaMashiach).

Secondly, as always, this book is dedicated to my beloved wife, the love of my life, my soul mate, Lady Krishana Haywood.

Thirdly, this book is dedicated to the people of the local assembly where I serve, Greater Christ Temple in Fort Wayne, Indiana. The very best saints that can be found. It is my pleasure to serve the LORD by serving you!

Contents

Section 01. Shift Into GREATER

CHAPTERS

Section 02. Work The SHIFT

CHAPTERS

Section 03. SHIFT The World

CHAPTERS

SECTION 1

CHAPTER 1

Chapter 1.
The Shift

"Not as though I had already attained, either were already perfect: but I follow after, if that I may apprehend that for which also I am apprehended of Christ Jesus. Brethren, I count not myself to have apprehended: but this one thing I do, forgetting those things which are behind, and reaching forth unto those things which are before, I press toward the mark for the prize of the high calling of God in Christ Jesus." (Philippians 3:12-14)

Shift = A change in position, direction, or tendency

- Change = To make the form, nature, content, or future course different from what is, has been, or currently is.

As we near the conclusion of those things inscribed in the Holy Scriptures concerning the end of this present age, one of the things most concerning to leaders who are tapped in to the heart of God is the spirit of complacency amongst the believers.

The mantra of “come as you are” has done much to secure an environment wherein guests and visitors feel comfortable enough to attend our worship services, however, it would seem that someone forgot to inform those who come and take hold of this most holy faith that once you have “come as you are” you are not intended to “remain as you have been”!

The western church in the twenty-first century surely suffers from delusions of grandeur. Perhaps it is our mass consumption of the hyper-grace heresy, the “it doesn’t matter what I do because I’m saved by God’s underserved mercy” cult which is producing carnal (read as un-saved) believers by the thousands. Perhaps it is due to just plain old lazy spirituality, either way the devil has pulled the wool over the eyes of many people.

The result is that we think once we have accepted Christ as our Lord and Savior, we are coasting into the Kingdom of Heaven with no need to grow in spirituality, that there is no real reason to strive for righteousness in our conduct, that there is no call to press toward the mark for the prize of the high calling of God in Jesus Christ.

How wrong we are.

Observe that the great theologian, the Apostle Paul himself, took the time to point out the fact that he was not yet perfected, but continued to strive for purity in every area of his life: "Not as though I had already attained, either were already perfect: but I follow after, if that I may apprehend that for which also I am apprehended of Christ Jesus".

Paul said, "I follow after", which is to say "I am in hot pursuit of the goal which is before me!" Paul is not lackadaisical, nor is he resting on his laurels. If anyone had something to be proud of, it most certainly would be the great Apostle Paul: "Though I might also have confidence in the flesh. If any other man thinketh that he hath whereof he might trust in the flesh, I more: Circumcised the eighth day, of the stock of Israel, of the tribe of Benjamin, an Hebrew of the Hebrews; as touching the law, a Pharisee; Concerning zeal, persecuting the church; touching the righteousness which is in the law, blameless." (Phil 3:4-6)

In addition to these things, Paul had a personal encounter with the post-resurrection Christ (Acts 9:1-5), a miraculous conversion, and was subsequently sent forth by the Holy Spirit with the laying on of the hands of the presbytery as an apostle in the Lord's Church. Surely if anyone could say they had "arrived" it would be Paul, but instead Paul says, ""Not as though I had already attained, either were already perfect: but I follow after, if that I may apprehend that for which also I am apprehended of Christ Jesus".

In other words, Paul was not satisfied with the level of relationship with the Spirit of the Almighty that he found himself at, but he decided that he must "follow after", which is to say that he must pursue, he must press in, he must make every effort to reach for another level in God. Paul had determined within himself that he would not rest at the dimension of faith that brought him into salvation, but that he yet desired to change for the better, to Shift into GREATER!

If ever we are to become what God would have us to truly be, we must undergo a radical transformation and be gripped by the call of God to shift into a different **position**, a different **direction**, and into different **tendencies**.

Position = a particular way in which someone or something is placed or arranged

I speak here of mental position. We are all born in sin and shaped in iniquity, we both come into this world with, and are trained through environment and experience to have a mind which is set (positioned) in sin.

Nobody had to teach little Johnny how to lie, but when his mother walks into the room and asks "Little Johnny, who ate the cookies?", with crumbs on his mouth and shirt, little Johnny replies, "I don't know, mommy."

We make our entrance into this existence with sin already accompanying us. This position, this mindset, is strengthened as we are encouraged by our entertainment, television, movies, magazines, music, etc., that sins such as lying and even petty theft are okay if we deem it to be necessary or even convenient.

From this position a person will never develop in Christ. After all, the scriptures tell us that Jesus came to save us FROM our sin (Matthew 1:21), He did not come to save us IN our sin.

To walk with Christ requires that we be willing to sacrifice our old self, our old ways, our old mindsets, and SHIFT into a new mental position. God is calling for a people who will not be conformed (shaped, molded) to this world, the current structure and ways of secular society, but will instead be transformed, changed, shifted, by the renewing of the mind. This renewing is like when a building is renovated, the building itself is not replaced, but is updated and receives new amenities. Just as the old building will see the outdated water fountains, tiles, and light fixtures torn out and tossed into the trash, only to be replaced by newer, up-to-date, and simply better versions, so must the believer cooperate as co-laborers with the Spirit of God to see their old vengefulness, un-forgiveness, violence, hatred, and bitterness replaced with love, joy, peace, grace, mercy, patience, and gentleness. The old mind must be reprogrammed to function with the mind of Christ. We must SHIFT into GREATER position!

Direction = a course along which someone or something moves.

The movement of our old lives, before we are redeemed, is toward the gates of hell. Everything in our environment and culture is intended to keep us moving in that same destructive direction. The direction of a person's movement will determine their ultimate destination. A man can tell you a thousand times that he's driving from Indianapolis, Indiana to Los Angeles, California, but if he gets in his car and begins driving toward the east, passing through Ohio while you continue to warn him of his wrong direction, cruising through Pennsylvania regardless of your constant pleas, he will eventually arrive at the east coast, the opposite of his stated destination, regardless of where his mouth has said he was going.

There are plenty of believers in Jesus Christ who state that they are on their way to heaven while living like hellions on earth. Jesus said in Matthew 7:21, "Not everyone who says to Me, 'Lord, Lord,' shall enter the kingdom of heaven, but he who does the will of My Father in heaven."

Though the doctrine of grace teaches us that we have not and could not earn or deserve the mercy and salvation of Jesus Christ, it is surely one of the biggest errors of our generation that leads so many to think that once a person has received the free gift of salvation, that person is not called upon and held responsible for changing the direction of their life by the help and guidance of the Holy Spirit. Nobody expects the new believer to bring forth complete and perfect compliance with the Word and will of God at all times, but, beyond all shadow of doubt, a person must set the goal of perfect performance in order to ever achieve excellent performance. It is satan who schemes to trick Christians into missing the mark of God's righteousness by causing us to aim too low. The marksman who aims for the outer circle will never hit the bullseye!

If you are to ever walk into the destiny that God dreamed of for you from the foundation of the world, you will have to SHIFT your life's direction:

"How shall we, that are dead to sin, live any longer therein?" (Romans 6:2)

Tendencies = an inclination toward a particular characteristic or type of behavior.

Jesus said “by their fruits you shall know them” (Matthew 7:20). Fruit is a natural outgrowth. It is what naturally proceeds from within. One need not purchase special vitamin enriched water, or sprinkle fairy dust and say an incantation to make apples grow out of an apple tree. If the tree is, in fact, an apple tree, and the tree is alive, apples will naturally come forth from its branches.

Jesus uses this agricultural reference to illustrate the fact that people also bear fruit. Just as a fruit tree is identified by the type of fruit that comes out of it, so are people revealed by what naturally proceeds from within them.

The most consistent way to measure the fruit of a person is to take note of one’s tendencies. Our tendencies are our most foundational habits that are not only formed by the repetition of our outward actions, but are also based in our internal position and direction.

The things that you naturally do and say are the overflow of what is in your heart (spirit): "Either make the tree good and its fruit good, or else make the tree bad and its fruit bad; for a tree is known by its fruit. Brood of vipers! How can you, being evil, speak good things? For out of the abundance of the heart the mouth speaks. A good man out of the good treasure of his heart brings forth good things, and an evil man out of the evil treasure brings forth evil things. (Matthew 12:33-36 NKJV)

CHAPTER 2

Chapter 2
Make The Shift

"In those days John the Baptist came preaching in the wilderness of Judea, and saying, "Repent, for the kingdom of heaven is at hand!" For this is he who was spoken of by the prophet Isaiah, saying: "The voice of one crying in the wilderness: 'Prepare the way of the Lord; Make His paths straight.'" Now John himself was clothed in camel's hair, with a leather belt around his waist; and his food was locusts and wild honey. Then Jerusalem, all Judea, and all the region around the Jordan went out to him 6 and were baptized by him in the Jordan, confessing their sins. But when he saw many of the Pharisees and Sadducees coming to his baptism, he said to them, "Brood of vipers! Who warned you to flee from the wrath to come? Therefore bear fruits worthy of repentance, and do not think to say to yourselves, 'We have Abraham as our father.' For I say to you that God is able to raise up children to Abraham from these stones. And even now the ax is laid to the root of the trees. Therefore every tree which does not bear good fruit is cut down and thrown into the fire." (Matthew 3:1-10)

Talk is cheap. A man promises his son that he will take him to the baseball game this weekend. The son's hopes are activated, he begins to dream of seeing the batter swinging for the fences and rounding the bases. He can almost smell the hotdogs. He tells his mom and his friends with maximum excitement. The weekend comes. Dad doesn't show up at all. It cost him nothing to make the promise, but the tickets are costly, and dad's check is short this week. The son is embarrassed and disappointed because he built and expectation based on words that were spoken. In the future, words become meaningless to him, because he has learned the hard way that words without action are worthless.

Politicians constantly make un-kept promises. "I will lower your taxes", "read my lips, no new taxes", "we will provide excellent education for everyone", etc.
It's easy to make any promise while on the campaign trail, but once a person gets into office, they find that doing what they promised is far more complicated than they expected. There are miles of red-tape and labyrinths of bureaucracy to navigate through, if the elected official even had an inclination to attempt the great feat of fulfilling their promises to begin with. The public is left disillusioned. Empty words and promises are of no value.

Religious people talk about what they believe, but don't connect it to their everyday conduct. Herein is the powerlessness of religiosity. To speak of Christ to family members and friends while failing to allow Christ to reign in your life is a dishonor to the Christ that we speak so highly of. Not only is this conduct non-fruitful, but it is anti-fruitful and anti-Christ, as hypocrisy is a major contributor to the difficulty found in our attempts to help people surrender themselves to Christ.

A hypocrite is an actor, one who wears a mask to conceal their true identity in order to temporarily play a part.
Not only do people have no use for others who speak empty words, but God Himself is repulsed by hypocrisy!
“For you were hypocrites in your hearts when you sent me to the Lord your God, saying, 'Pray for us to the Lord our God, and according to all that the Lord your God says, so declare to us and we will do it.' And I have this day declared it to you, but you have not obeyed the voice of the Lord your God, or anything which He has sent you by me. Now therefore, know certainly that you shall die by the sword, by famine, and by pestilence in the place where you desire to go to dwell." (Jeremiah 42:20-22)
Here the great prophet Jeremiah says “you were hypocrites when you said to me that you would do whatever God commanded, because I declared His word to you and you did not obey it. For this reason you will die by sword, famine, and pestilence…” (*paraphrase mine*).

A relationship with people cannot be cultivated with words alone, neither can a person progress in a relationship with the Almighty unless their words and actions become integrated. Our status with God is not based on what we claim to believe, but on whether or not we allow our beliefs to be made manifest in our conduct.

In Matthew 7:20 Jesus said that "by their fruits ye shall know them". Fruit is a natural outgrowth. If you have an apple tree that is alive, apples will naturally grow out of it. You don't need to do anything special to make this happen. The apple is a natural outgrowth of the apple tree. Your fruit is what naturally comes out of you. Your deeds, conduct, behavior, and actions, these things are the evidence of who you truly are! Your response to the situations and circumstances of life reveal what is in your heart (spirit), "for out of the abundance of the heart, the mouth speaketh" (Matthew 12:34).

God desires to bring about a radical transformation in your life, but He will not change you without your consent and cooperation. The shift that God is leading you into requires your decision and active follow through. Your destiny is waiting for you to Make The SHIFT!

CHAPTER 3

Chapter 3
Activating Destiny

"For thus says the Lord: After seventy years are completed at Babylon, I will visit you and perform My good word toward you, and cause you to return to this place. For I know the thoughts that I think toward you, says the Lord, thoughts of peace and not of evil, to give you a future and a hope." (Jeremiah 29:10-11)

God's desire for your life is that He might bless you, and prosper you, and let the glory of His presence rest on you. The Almighty is a loving Father, as such, He desires every good thing for His children. "Do not fear, little flock, for it is your Father's good pleasure to give you the kingdom." (Luke 32:32)

God is not a mean, old, white haired, man in the sky who's waiting to hit you with a thunderbolt the first moment you go astray. That image which has been hoisted upon the minds of the masses is, in fact, Zeus. Jehovah is not a vindictive tyrant who waits with baited breath for the opportunity to strike you down. Rather, the true God of heaven and earth is patient, the chief exemplar of longsuffering. He is supremely merciful in dealing with humanity. Keep in mind that we are certainly guilty of breaking the divine law in every way, yet, in spite of our overflowing iniquity, He grants us access to speak to Him directly in confessing our sin and asking for forgiveness as we forsake them.

God doesn't desire anyone's destruction, but He waits patiently giving us all a chance to turn from our rebellion and embrace Him, "The Lord is not slack concerning His promise, as some count slackness, but is longsuffering toward us, not willing (desiring) that any should perish but that all should come to repentance." (2 Peter 3:9).

Consider that, God's people, the nation of Israel, entered the promise land in 1400 BC, and failed to serve God with their whole hearts repeatedly, and went after other gods repeatedly, until finally, because of their persistence in sin, God exiled them from the promise land by allowing Nebuchadnezzar to take them as captives into Babylon. God waited for Israel to repent and be faithful, He waited for 795 years, during which time Israel continually backslid into worshipping the baalim, the gods of Babylon.

Yet God still says to them, “I know the thoughts that I think toward you”, present tense, “think”. How incredible, the average person would write off someone who is unfaithful, yet the Almighty doesn’t say, “the thoughts that I **thought** toward you”, which would mean that I **did** think to bless you, but not anymore. No, instead, by saying “the thoughts that I **think** toward you”, He shows that, despite Israel’s persistence in disobedience, He **continuously** thinks thoughts of blessing toward them, to give them a future and a hope!

God, in like manner, is patient with you, as He was with Israel, because He has a plan for you, as He did for Israel. He has a destiny for you. God had a vision of the perfect you before the foundation of the world, and He is dedicated to bringing that perfect version of you out of the current version of you.

God’s idea of destiny is not like man’s.
Webster’s dictionary: “Destiny” = the predetermined or inevitable course of events considered beyond the power or control of people.
God’s concept of destiny is the fulfillment of His perfect will for your life, that you would operate in your divine purpose, that you would know the joy of walking in His eternal design

for your life, His blessing and favor on your temporal life, and your ultimate salvation, eternal life in His presence!

To get to destiny from where we are now requires a shifting in our lives. God, contrary to popular belief, will not bring about the necessary changes within an individual all by Himself. He certainly could, but He has chosen to be a co-laborer with you for your own development. This means that God has a shift for your spirit, but you are responsible to Activate the SHIFT!

4 SHIFTS to prepare you for DESTINY:

1) Perception
2) Process
3) Procedure
4) Production

1) Shift your Perceptions

- You must view things differently…

We must move from a temporal outlook to viewing the events and circumstances of life from the eternal perspective, through the eyes of Christ. Your outlook frames

your thought processes. All things are interpreted by the preset configurations that you have set in your mind.
In order to achieve any meaningful level of transformation in your life, it will be necessary to abandon your previously

entrenched perceptions in order to obtain a new way of viewing life and the events thereof.

It is often noted that God moves in mysterious ways. This is a derivative of the scriptural statement from God, “For My thoughts are not your thoughts, Nor are your ways My ways," says the Lord. "For as the heavens are higher than the earth, So are My ways higher than your ways, And My thoughts than your thoughts.” (Isaiah 55:8-9)

If ever we are, at any level, to understand the ways of God, we must determine to look and understand from the eternal perspective. It is a carnal mind, the mind which is consumed by the temporal things of this world, that blocks the eyes of our understanding. For this reason we are beckoned by the Spirit of God to dwell in the secret place and abide under the shadow of the Almighty.

To dwell in the secret place is to live with a spiritual mind and outlook. Rather than simply visiting the splendiferous presence of God in our weekly worship services, only to return to mundane existence throughout the week, we are invited to abide, to take up residence in the very presence of our Creator. Hallelujah!

2) Shift your Process

- You must think about things differently…

Everything begins with your thinking process. Your thoughts are manifested as words, your words a proven through action, your actions develop into habits, your habits define your character, and your character determines your destination. In order to walk in divine destiny, putting off the old man and being clothed about in the new man, one must begin by seeking to be renewed in the spirit of their mind (see Ephesians 4:20-24).

"And do not be conformed to this world, but be transformed by the renewing of your mind, that you may prove what is that good and acceptable and perfect will of God."
(Romans 12:2)

Being conformed to this world, or to any system for that matter, is a result of the programming you undergo from the beginning of life until the moment of your last breath.

This programming happens by way of what you receive through the gates of your soul, meaning your eyes and ears. The things you observe and listen to have a much more profound effect on your life than the average person understands. Everything you receive through your gates contributes to your subconscious makeup and factors into your overall personality. In order to shift your process, you will need to shift your intake. A person who desires to stop cussing will do well to stop watching cussing television and movies, as well as to stop listening to cussing music.

A person who wants to be delivered from a spirit of lust should begin by cutting off their intake of sexualized entertainment, movies, television, radio, magazines.

Replace these things with the Word of God and prayer.

Wholesome intake begets wholesome output. You will only do what is in your heart and mind, you will only speak what is in your heart and mind.

"...For out of the abundance of the heart the mouth speaks." (Matthew 12:34)

Once you have changed what you put into your inner man, you can begin to shift how you process the outer world in your mind.

A citizen of the kingdom must think of things differently than a person of the temporal world. A Kingdom citizen isn't an enemy to anyone, though others may position themselves as enemies to them. If I think of myself as your enemy I will treat you as an enemy. If I think of you as a confused potential ally, I will treat you with kindness though you haven't yet learned that I am your friend.

This is the mindset required in Romans chapter 12:
“Repay no one evil for evil. Have regard for good things in the sight of all men. If it is possible, as much as depends on you, live peaceably with all men. Beloved, do not avenge yourselves, but rather give place to wrath; for it is written, "Vengeance is Mine, I will repay," says the Lord. Therefore
"If your enemy is hungry, feed him;
If he is thirsty, give him a drink;
For in so doing you will heap coals of fire on his head."
Do not be overcome by evil, but overcome evil with good.
(Romans 12:17-21)

3) Shift your Procedure

- You must respond to things differently…

We must begin to actively implement the Word of God in our everyday situations. Blessing does not proceed from how much truth a person knows, but from how much truth a person applies in their life.

Whereas in former times, when my boss would give me a difficult time, and I felt that it was unfair, I would begin grumble and fuss, rip down labels and kick machines. I would talk about the boss behind his back and generally produce, or further fee into, a negative atmosphere in my work environment.
This behavior did nothing to fix the issues at hand, neither did it present a good Christian example for my coworkers.

I could not control the circumstances that led to my displeasure, however, I always have control of my response to the situations and circumstances of life. If my desire is to grow deeper in God and reach higher in destiny, I find that purposefully shifting my procedure of response is thoroughly indispensable to my goal. Not only is this proactive correction necessary for the maintenance of my own internal peace, but, keeping in mind the responsibility of evangelism which is given to all of the saints, it is key in representing Christ as He truly is so that others might gain faith in Him through seeing the real change that God has produced in your life.

I encourage you to the make a decision, to take a stand this very day and declare to yourself, "I will not respond as I once did, I choose to shift my procedure!"

4) Shift your Production

- You must initiate things differently…

Not only is it important to learn to respond differently to the things that life throws at us, but we must also learn to initiate things differently than we have in the past.
Your attitude and presentation has a tremendous influence on the effectiveness of your various endeavors.

A wife opens the front door of the house. She walks in silently, she doesn't make eye contact with her husband. She doesn't make small talk about how her day was, nor does she ask her husband how his day was. She takes off her winter coat, hangs it in the hall closet, drops her purse on the dining room table and proceeds directly to the bedroom where she summarily shuts the door.
Tension has just been created. Her husband can feel the frigidity in the atmosphere. Her mind is actually consumed in the difficulties of her day, but her husband assumes that

she is still stewing from the argument of last night. As a result he carries out an entire new argument in his head before approaching his wife. As they engage the assumptions mount and boil over into screaming. The verbal altercation is completely unnecessary and avoidable, but both the husband and wife have initiated incorrectly and the result is an unfavorable production (the argument about nothing).

How you begin a thing will greatly determine the outcome. In order to arrive at blessing, growth, effectiveness, and development, one will need to submit to the flow of God's Spirit concerning how we initiate things.
"Commit your works to the Lord, and your thoughts will be established." (Proverbs 16:3)

3 Keys to Activating Your Destiny:

1) Stop Self Destructive Behavior
2) Speak the Word
3) Put the Word into ACTION

Key #1 Stop Self Destructive Behavior

"When I shut up heaven and there is no rain, or command the locusts to devour the land, or send pestilence among My people, if My people who are called by My name will humble themselves, and pray and seek My face, and turn from their wicked ways, then I will hear from heaven, and will forgive their sin and heal their land." (2 Chronicles 7:13-14)

If you know you are in sin, God will sometimes send calamity your way in order to get your attention and call you to TURN BACK!

Let us recognize that God is speaking to us, through both blessings and curses. Say what? Can a Spirit-filled believer be cursed? YES! With all absoluteness I tell you that, according to the holy writ, disobedience to God brings The Curse on anyone!

"But it shall come to pass, if you do not obey the voice of the Lord your God, to observe carefully all His commandments and His statutes which I command you today, that all these curses will come upon you and overtake you: "Cursed shall you be in the city, and cursed shall you be in the country. "Cursed shall be your basket and your kneading bowl. "Cursed shall be the fruit of your body and the produce of your land, the increase of your cattle and the offspring of your flocks. "Cursed shall you be when you come in, and cursed shall you be when you go out. "The Lord will send on you cursing, confusion, and rebuke in all that you set your hand to do, until you are destroyed and until you perish quickly, because of the wickedness of your doings in which you have forsaken Me." (Deuteronomy 28:15-21)

The call to salvation is the call to change. Transformation can't occur as long as a person is set within themselves to continue in the same self-destructive behavior after the cross that they were engaged in before the cross.
You won't enter the next level while you're still lying, you won't succeed while you're still stealing, you won't be victorious while you're still being violent!

The blessing of the LORD requires that a person lives out the principle of repentance. Repentance is not an apology, it's a CHANGE in your mind and behavior by God's help!
Many people decide to commit sin, thinking "I will repent afterward", this foolishness is a deception birthed in the depths of hell. This very satanic mindset is what traps many nominal Christians outside of the blessings of God and blocks their access to true purpose and destiny.

Repentance is the decision to change your behavior by changing your mind. The Greek word "metanoia", which is translated as "repent", means beyond the mind, above the mind, transcend the mind, or transformed mind. Every action begins in the mind. It is impossible to transform the behavior without undergoing a radical transformation of the mind by the Holy Spirit!

Repentance requires that a person acknowledge their own sin, and make the decision to abandon that mindset, action, and lifestyle, and pursue a life of faithful obedience to God through trusting in His Holy Spirit.

"He who covers his sins will not prosper,
But whoever confesses and forsakes them will have mercy."
(Proverbs 28:13)

Key #2 Speak the Word

Faith comes by hearing, and hearing by the Word of God. This principle is even more effective when the one you hear speaking the Word of God is yourself!

In my years as a salesman, working on full commission, I was taught that one of the most powerful selling tools is the concept of getting people to say that they need it with their own mouths. Simply stated, you may doubt what I say, especially when you know I'm trying to sell you something, but you will always believe yourself. Based on this theory, we were taught to demonstrate the products, then ask the customer if they would agree that the product would increase their quality of life in whatever capacity the particular product was designed to do so. Having just cut a coin in half with the most amazing scissors you've ever seen, or having just sucked sixty pads of dirt out of the carpet that you've just vacuumed before I arrived, or otherwise demonstrated the supreme superiority of whatever product we are selling, the customer would be nearly forced to admit that this is better than what they already have, and that obtaining this product would increase their quality of life. However, the product is not sold until the customer says, with their own mouth, that they want and need this product. With this in mind, we were trained to, not only demonstrate a superior product, but to also ask questions along the way to which the customer would almost certainly have to answer with a "yes". The course of sixty or so "yes" questions, in combo with the demonstration, would ultimately culminate with the customer saying "Yes, I need this product". Once the customer had spoken these words, or some similar phrase, the sale is over. Once a person hears their self say that something is true, it now becomes really true to them.

The principle is powerful when applied to the Word of God. I encourage you to read the Word of God out-loud. When you hear your own voice speaking the holy Word, your psyche accepts it as reality more quickly and begins the process of assimilating this truth into your everyday life! This is also why it is important to be in the house of worship when the Word is going forth. God has given us preachers and teachers to declare the whole counsel of God in our hearing. One of the chief purposes of attending both Sunday morning worship and also Bible study is so that our soul will be fed and strengthened, and so that faith, the rock solid trust in God which results in corresponding action, will be birthed within us.

Every time you hear His Word, your faith is increased and you are empowered to DO His Word! When I hear the Word of God, I am reminded that with God all things are possible. I am reminded that I can do all things through Christ who strengthens me. I am reminded that He is the LORD who gives me the power to get wealth, the LORD my healer, the LORD my shepherd, the LORD my banner of victory, etc.

But if faith comes by hearing, then the opposite of faith, which is fear, also comes by hearing and hearing by any other word beside God's. If you want to walk more mightily in the Spirit of God, you must shut out the words of doubt, fear, and failure which are declared to you through the hellavision and the radio, through magazines and popular culture, and, instead, fill yourself with the Word of God by reading, studying, hearing, and meditating on the Word of the living God. We weaken faith by listening to the wrong sources, and even more so when we accept their grim prognostications and begin to speak them with our own mouths.

Stop saying what man has said, start saying what God has said!

"I shall not die, but live, and declare the works of the Lord." (Psalm 118:17)

By speaking His Word YHWH created the universe and gave order to it, by speaking His Word you call this world in chaos to return to her proper order that was set by God.

"By faith we understand that the worlds were framed by the word of God, so that the things which are seen were not made of things which are visible." (Hebrews 11:3)

By speaking His Word you can discontinue disease.

"...by His stripes we are healed." (Isaiah 53:5)

By speaking His Word you can bring peace into a tense environment.

“Then He arose and rebuked the wind, and said to the sea, "Peace, be still!" And the wind ceased and there was a great calm.” (Mark 4:39-40)

By speaking His Word you can dislodge demons...
“For He said to him, "Come out of the man, unclean spirit!" (Mark 5:8)

By speaking His Word you can SHIFT the atmosphere...
“And Elijah the Tishbite, of the inhabitants of Gilead, said to Ahab,"As the Lord God of Israel lives, before whom I stand, there shall not be dew nor rain these years, except at my word." (1 Kings 17:1)

Key #3 Put the Word into Action

Faith without works is dead. (James 2:26)

Dead, in this text means fruitless, void, empty, powerless, useless, and worthless.
BELIEF does not become FAITH until it is manifested through ACTIONS!

Jesus became famous throughout all of Israel for healing all manner of diseases, making the lame walk, making the deaf hear, and making the blind see. He was called to the house of Jairus whose daughter was sick unto death, "But as He went, the multitudes thronged Him. 43Now a woman, having a flow of blood for twelve years, who had spent all her livelihood on physicians and could not be healed by any, 44came from behind and touched the border of His garment. And immediately her flow of blood stopped." (Luke 8:42-44)

This woman was bleeding for twelve years! The Bible tells us that the LIFE of the flesh is in the BLOOD (Leviticus 17:11)! For twelve long years the very LIFE was being drained out of her! Scholars believe the issue is one of fibroid tumors, this kind of tumor develops in your reproductive system and blocks your ability to bring forth and produce children! For twelve long years this woman was fruitless! This woman spent all of her life's saving on human doctors who couldn't heal her issue!

Her condition made her ceremonially unclean, and anyone she touched would be considered unclean, an offense that she could be stoned to death for.

When she heard about Jesus Christ the healer, she got up and left her house, she pushed her way through the crowd, and, against all odds, she took hold of the hem of His garment and was HEALED!

She wasn't healed by sitting by and believing for a healing, she was healed when she believed for a healing and ACTED on what she believed! You have to put the Word into action!

SECTION 2

CHAPTER 4

Chapter 4
Meditation

"This Book of the Law shall not depart from your mouth, but you shall meditate in it day and night, that you may observe to do according to all that is written in it. For then you will make your way prosperous, and then you will have good success." (Joshua 1:8)

Before the shift of God's Spirit can be made manifest outwardly, it must be made inwardly. In this section we will discuss the fundamentals of spiritual development that will allow you to cooperate with the shift that God is bringing about in your soul.

The first principle we will discuss is meditation. This meditation is not the eastern meditation of Hinduism and other like religious traditions. Eastern religions practice meditation in order to empty the mind in order to become "one with the universe" or to "realize the divinity within". The danger of this concept is that the spirits behind it want you to empty your mind so that they can fill it with something. Eastern meditation is basically a technique of allowing unclean spirits to fill your soul. The meditation of the bible is not intended to empty the mind, but quite the opposite, to fill the mind.

The Hebrew word translated into English as meditate is "hagah", which means to mutter, to mumble, to repeat to one's self under the breath. The concept being communicated is the idea of not just reading the Word of God, but repeating it to yourself continually, muttering it under your breath, thinking on hit, ruminating on it, contemplating on it, concentrating on it, praying it, speaking it in conversation, researching it, and seeking to understand it in all of its manifold splendor.

In Joshua chapter one, verse eight, God instructed Israel's new leader, Joshua, that "This book of the Law shall not depart from your mouth…". This is to say that the Word of God should continually be in your mouth. You should continue to speak it, even when only speaking to yourself (hagah) in order that the Word might become implanted into your subconscious mind where it will affect your habits and contribute to the development of your character. *"Therefore lay aside all filthiness and overflow of wickedness, and receive with meekness the **implanted** word, which is able to save your souls."* (James 1:21)

The passage goes on to say, "but you shall meditate in it day and night". You shall allow the Word of God, His commands, instructions, dictates, statutes, prophecies, and promises to be repeated both in your mouth and in your heart continuously throughout your day. This is intended to drive the Word into your inner man, your subconscious mind, which is the control center of your life. Jesus said, *"A good man out of the good treasure of his heart brings forth good; and an evil man out of the evil treasure of his heart brings forth evil. For out of the abundance of the heart his mouth speaks."* (Luke 6:45) A persons speaks (and acts) according to what is already in their heart (inner man, subconscious mind). There is much depth in what Jesus has said here, a person cannot live contrary to what is in their deepest parts. The subconscious mind (heart), being the control center of your life, is the determining factor of your behavior. This means you can make a decision with your conscious mind to behave differently, and you may have some success as long as you are focused and concentrating on behaving differently, but as soon as your mind is occupied by anything else you will act according to your preset programming. Your subconscious mind is the house of habits, feelings, emotions, and instincts. When you are operating on auto-pilot, you are functioning by the subconscious mind (heart).

The purpose of scriptural meditation is to change the programming of the subconscious mind (heart) by repetition, which is the same way it was programmed to start with. All of our unredeemed lives we are fed a steady stream of godless thoughts and behaviors, these are strengthened by the television, movies, magazines and especially the music we accept through our gates (eyes and ears). These things go in our eye and ear gates and settle into the heart (subconscious mind), where they form the framework of our thought lives. From these frameworks we take action in various situations, and when repeated they form our habits. Our habits define our character, and our character determines our destination. If I want to have a positive destination, I must change the root, my thought life, by changing what I allow into my heart (subconscious mind).

As a person continues to recondition the mind by meditating in the Word of God, the Word is both repeated in the mind in order to speak it, and repeated in the ears as a result of speaking it, which leads to a strengthening of resolve, confidence, and faith in God's Word.

"So then faith comes by hearing, and hearing by the word of God." (Romans 10:17)

God goes on to tell Joshua that the purpose in this meditative practice is that he might *"observe to do all that is written in it"* (the Word).

We don't engage in the practice of scriptural meditation simply for the sake of being able to say that we meditate in the Word, nor do we for simply the idea of filling the mind (heart) with God's Word, but for the outcome that, having filled the heart (subconscious mind) with the Word of God, we will be sufficiently transformed by the renewing of the mind so that we might actually do the Word instead of being hearers only.

"But be doers of the word, and not hearers only, deceiving yourselves." (James 1:22-23)

God's blessing rests upon those who activate the Word of God in their lives through scriptural meditation and real time implementation.

"...for then you will make your way prosperous, and then you will have good success." (Joshua 1:8)

CHAPTER 5

Chapter 5.
Prayer

"Be anxious for nothing, but in everything by prayer and supplication, with thanksgiving, let your requests be made known to God; and the peace of God, which surpasses all understanding, will guard your hearts and minds through Christ Jesus." (Philippians 4:6-7)

Prayer, which comes from the Greek word "proseuche", is "communion with God".

Through prayer we actually experience relationship with God. The quality of our prayer life then determines the quality of our relationship with God. Prayer is talking **with** God (not talking to God, or talking at God). Prayer includes **listening** to God.

Prayer is enjoying the presence of God. It takes many forms, for example: praise, confession, thanksgiving, petition (asking for things), waiting (silent listening and sensing God) and warfare, we even have the privilege of praying with the Spirit in a language unknown to us.

Prayer is not simply saying words. It is not repeating formulas. God is looking for passionate relationship and heartfelt communication:

"...The **earnest** prayer of a **righteous** person has **great power** and produces **wonderful results**."
(James 5:16-17 NLT)

God does not respond to a person who attempts to use prayer like a magic formula or incantation (spells, witchcraft):

"And when you pray, do not use vain repetitions as the heathen *do*. For they think that they will be heard for their many words. "Therefore do not be like them. For your Father knows the things you have need of before you ask Him." (Matthew 6:7-8)

There is, unfortunately, much so called "prayer" that never reaches God:

"One who turns away his ear from hearing the law,
Even his prayer *is* an abomination." (Proverbs 28:9)

Prayer, then, is when a person who has been clothed with the righteousness of Christ makes **heartfelt** communication with God, including both **speaking to God** and **listening to God**, thusly, cultivating a **relationship** with God through true **communion** (common union) with God.

Communion is Joint participation, fellowship, the sharing or exchanging of intimate thoughts and feelings, especially when the exchange is on a mental or spiritual level.

<u>Why Do I Need To Pray?</u>

1. We pray because we love God.

We spend time with God in prayer and communication because we love Him.

Just as a man and woman who are in love desire to be together and communicate, so we, if we love God, will desire to be with Him and to fellowship with Him in proportion to our love for Him.

2. We pray because we depend on God. God is our source.

He is our life (Colossians 3:4). Through prayer we receive the comfort, the strength and all the other resources that we need in life – both naturally and spiritually.
Prayer (relationship to God) is as necessary to spiritual life as oxygen is to natural life.

3. We need to pray in order to resist temptation.

Much sin is the result of prayerlessness:
"Watch and pray, lest you enter into temptation. The spirit indeed *is* willing, but the flesh *is* weak." (Matthew 26:41)

4. We need to pray because it is necessary for people to invite God to act in salvation.

Satan is actively blinding the minds of mankind to the gospel, teaching our youth to doubt anything biblical, and pushing for legislation that will stop Christians from being able to share their faith anywhere. It is necessary that we combat this strategy with prayers that God will open a door for the gospel and cause it to be effective:

"Finally, brethren, pray for us, that the word of the Lord may run *swiftly* and be glorified, just as *it is* with you, and that we may be delivered from unreasonable and wicked men; for not all have faith." (2 Thessalonians 3:1-2)

"meanwhile praying also for us, that God would open to us a door for the word, to speak the mystery of Christ, for which I am also in chains" (Colossians 4:3)

5. We need to pray because God commands us to pray.

"Then He spoke a parable to them, that men always ought to pray and not lose heart" (Luke 18:1)

"pray without ceasing" (1 Thessalonians 5:17)

Prayer is so vital to all that God wants to do on the earth, and so essential to us, that God commands us to do it all the time! We should even deny ourselves sleep and food sometimes in order to pray more and with greater power. (Luke 6:12/Luke 21:36/Colossians 4:2)

<u>Types of Prayer</u>

Praise * Thanksgiving * Petition * Intercession * Warfare

<u>Praise</u>: The expression of appreciation for who God is and/or His attributes.

"Praise the LORD! For *it is* good to sing praises to our God; For *it is* pleasant, *and* praise is beautiful." (Psalm 147:1)

We offer praise not because God needs it, rather, it is primarily for our benefit because our perspective changes. Praise reminds us of how powerful and loving God is, and, thusly, counteracts our tendency to reduce Him to being simply our butler. Praise prayers cause our eyes to open to the fact that we are not prisoners of our circumstances and that we are not the "victim", but instead because of Christ we are the "victors"!

<u>Thanksgiving</u>: The expression of appreciation for what God has done.
We must remember and express gratitude for what God has

given us – primarily the great blessing of salvation, and then also the temporal blessings He grants us.

"And let the peace of God rule in your hearts, to which also you were called in one body; and be thankful. Let the word of Christ dwell in you richly in all wisdom, teaching and admonishing one another in psalms and hymns and spiritual songs, singing with grace in your hearts to the Lord. And *whatever* you do in word or deed, *do* all in the name of the Lord Jesus, giving thanks to God the Father through Him." (Colossians 3:15-17)

Thanksgiving keeps us "sane" because we are, in fact, lavishly and incredibly blessed even though we truly deserved God's wrath.

Petition: Asking God to meet our personal needs, "give us this day our daily bread"

"Be anxious for nothing, but in everything by prayer and supplication, with thanksgiving, let your requests be made known to God" (Philippians 4:6)

Seeing as God already knows what we need before we ask Him (Matthew 6:8), we naturally wonder "why do we need to ask Him?"

The answer is, because this is the most basic and practical way in which we express dependence on God. When we pray, we acknowledge that we are helpless to do even the most basic things in life, and we affirm God's omnipotence (limitless power). This is worship, this is saying "God, you are greater than I am, and I **NEED** YOU!"

Intercession: Praying for others.
Intercede: from the Latin words, "inter" (between) and "cedere" (go). Meaning to "go between".

Through intercessory prayer we ask God to help people in ways that we cannot (encourage, convict, protect, save, heal, deliver).

As Christians we are to bear one another's burdens through prayer.

"Bear one another's burdens, and so fulfill the law of Christ." (Galatians 6:2)

The "law of Christ" is AGAPE (sacrificial) love. When we pray for each other we are placing someone else ahead of ourselves, which is exactly what was required of Christ.

All lastingly fruitful ministry begins with intercessory prayer:

"Finally, brethren, pray for us, that the word of the Lord may run *swiftly* and be glorified, just as *it is* with you"
(2 Thessalonians 3:1)

<u>Warfare Prayer</u>: Enforcing the rule and judgments of God through faith.

Several things take place during warfare prayer:

1. The believer must recognize that the problem, the enemy, and the battle is spiritual.

2. The believer must recognize and take hold of the authority of God which has been given to him/her through Christ.

   "Behold, I give you the authority to trample on serpents and scorpions, and over all the power of the enemy, and nothing shall by any means hurt you." (Luke 10:19)

3. The believer must speak the word (judgments) of God concerning a thing
   "And take the helmet of salvation, and the sword of the Spirit, which is the word of God" (Ephesians 6:17)

This causes several things to happen:

- The Word is heard in the believer's own ears thusly causing faith in God to arise in the heart of the believer.
  "So then faith comes by hearing, and hearing by the word of God. (Romans 10:17)

- The Word (Spirit, presence) of God is brought into the situation which immediately brings liberation from the enemy and all of his tactics.
  "Now the Lord is the Spirit; and where the Spirit of the Lord is, there is liberty." (2 Corinthians 3:17)

- The believer, having first recognized the need of God's help, and in submission to God, resists the devil by speaking God's Word and the devil is FORCED to flee:

  "Therefore submit to God. Resist the devil and he will flee from you." (James 4:7)

4. The believer must begin to praise and thank God for the victory though it is not yet manifested.
"Now thanks be to God who always leads us in triumph in Christ, and through us diffuses the fragrance of His knowledge in every place."
(2 Corinthians 2:14)

The Model Prayer

Christ instructed His disciples how to pray, it was not a prayer to be repeated as if it were a magical formula, but rather, a blueprint or guideline for prayer:

"In this manner, therefore, pray: Our Father in heaven, Hallowed be Your name. Your kingdom come. Your will be done on earth as *it is* in heaven. Give us this day our daily bread. And forgive us our debts, as we forgive our debtors. And do not lead us into temptation, but deliver us from the evil one. For Yours is the kingdom and the power and the glory forever. Amen. **(**Matthew 6:9-13)

- **Our Father in heaven**: We recognize that God is not like us, He is "other than", He is above us, heaven is his throne and earth is His foot-stool. - Acts 7:49

- **Hallowed be your name**: "May Your name be glorified and held as holy amongst all men". It is also to say that His name is hollowed (held as holy) to the person who is praying, thusly, this is praise.

- **Your kingdom come**: "May all the earth recognize Your authority to rule", also, "please let Your power be made manifest that others might know that the Kingdom of God is amongst men".

  This is submission to the will of God, which is worship.

- **Your will be done on earth as it is in heaven**: In heaven God's will is carried out immediately, this is praying that men would submit themselves to God's will immediately, as the angels do, and walk in the righteousness of Christ. It is also a petition for help in submitting to God's will in our own lives.

- **Give us this day our daily bread**: This is the petition for our daily sustenance. Once again it shows a dependence on God as one who is my mightier and more capable than yourself.

- **And forgive us our debts as we forgive our debtors:** This must necessarily involve the confession of our debts (transgressions) and the willful forgiving of those who have transgressed against us.

  We must treat others with the same love, grace, and mercy that God allows for us.

- **And do not lead us into temptation but deliver us from the evil one:** This is the petition for the Lord's help in living the Christian life, surely none of us can walk with Christ except by the help of the Holy Spirit.

  This also takes us into the realm of spiritual warfare as we pray against the devil, "but deliver us from the evil one".

- **For yours is the kingdom, and the power, and the glory forever:** Christ ends the prayer with praise and adoration, the confession of the superiority of God. Truly the rulership of heaven and earth (the Kingdom) belongs to God.

  All power belongs to God because He is omnipotent (all powerful / Elohim = powers).

  All glory, honor, and praise belongs to God, this is a statement of humility as opposed to the pride exhibited by Lucifer (Satan) who wanted all glory, honor, and praise for himself.

A.C.T.S.

Adoration **C**onfession **T**hanksgiving **S**upplication

And remember to

P.U.S.H.

Pray **U**ntil **S**omething **H**appens

“Pray without ceasing.” – 1 Thessalonians 5:17

CHAPTER 6

Chapter 6.
Fasting

"Consecrate a fast, call a sacred assembly;
Gather the elders and all the inhabitants of the land into the house of the Lord your God, and cry out to the Lord."
(Joel 1:14)

"Fast" comes from the Greek word, "Nesteuo", which means abstain from food (religiously)

Fasting is abstaining from food and/or drink for religious reasons and purposes. These reasons vary according to the situation wherein a fast is invoked.
Let us look at how fasting has been used in the bible:

"Lament like a virgin girded with sackcloth For the husband of her youth. The grain offering and the drink offering Have been cut off from the house of the LORD; The priests mourn, who minister to the LORD. The field is wasted, The land mourns; For the grain is ruined, The new wine is dried up, The oil fails. Be ashamed, you farmers, Wail, you vinedressers, For the wheat and the barley; Because the harvest of the field has perished. The vine has dried up, And the fig tree has withered; The pomegranate tree, The palm tree also, And the apple tree — All the trees of the field are withered; Surely joy has withered away from the sons of men. Gird yourselves and lament, you priests; Wail, you who minister before the altar; Come, lie all night in sackcloth, You who minister to my God; For the grain offering and the drink offering. Sanctify ye a fast, call a solemn assembly, gather the elders and all the inhabitants of the land into the house of the LORD your God, and cry unto the LORD" (Joel 1:8-14)

In the Old Testament fasting was used primarily as a means of outwardly showing one's repentance. When a person's actions prove the truth of their words, God moves. When the Apostle Paul preached, he instructed men, women, boys, girls, Jews, and Gentiles that they should repent, turn to God, and do works which are fit for repentance (Act 26:20), let the thief steal no more, let the liar lie no more.

Fasting is one way of showing God your sorrow over your sins by denying yourself, this self-imposed affliction was usually coupled with self-humiliation, as they both fasted and wore sackcloth for clothes.

Let us remember, the practice changes but the principle stands forever. We ought to be willing to change our ways and humble ourselves before the LORD our God.

This use of fasting is, however, not the best way, there is a fast known as “the fast of the LORD”, let us look into what it is, and what it’s purpose is:

> “Why have we fasted,' *they say,* 'and You have not seen? *Why* have we afflicted our souls, and You take no notice?' "In fact, in the day of your fast you find pleasure, And exploit all your laborers. Indeed you fast for strife and debate, And to strike with the fist of wickedness. You will not fast as *you do* this day, To make your voice heard on high. Is it a fast that I have chosen, A day for a man to afflict his soul? *Is it* to bow down his head like a bulrush, And to spread out sackcloth and ashes? Would you call this a fast, And an acceptable day to the LORD? "*Is* this not the fast that I have chosen: To loose the bonds of wickedness, To undo the heavy burdens, To let the oppressed go free and that you break every yoke? Is it not to share your bread with the hungry, and that you bring to your house the poor who are cast out; When you see the naked, that you cover him, and not hide yourself from your own flesh?” ” (Isa 58:3-7)

Let’s examine this text verse by verse:

- <u>Vs. 3</u>
  “Why have we fasted,' *they say,* 'and You have not seen? *Why* have we afflicted our souls, and You take

no notice?' "In fact, in the day of your fast you find pleasure, And exploit all your laborers."

- The people, here, are accusing God of ignoring their fasts, but God counters that, though they are abstaining from food and drink, still they are, in fact, not fasting because while they are abstaining from food and drink, they are, at the same time, behaving wickedly. They were fasting merely as a religious observance, but their hearts were not in it, so God responded to the actual condition of their hearts instead of their pious action.

- "Behold, the LORD's hand is not shortened, That it cannot save; Nor His ear heavy,That it cannot hear. But your iniquities have separated you from your God; And your sins have hidden *His* face from you, So that He will not hear." (Isaiah 59:1-2)

- Vs. 4
  "Indeed you fast for strife and debate, And to strike with the fist of wickedness. You will not fast as *you do* this day, To make your voice heard on high."

- They began to call a fast in order to strike their enemies with an affliction, they would simply then pretend to observe the fast themselves.

- This also involves fasting and praying that God might hear your prayers that you would prosper from wickedness, NONESENSE. You shall not fast like this!

- Vs. 5
  "Is it a fast that I have chosen, A day for a man to afflict his soul? *Is it* to bow down his head like a bulrush, And to spread out sackcloth and ashes? Would you call this a fast, And an acceptable day to the LORD?"

  - Has God even called us to the fast of repentance? Is this what He would prefer from us? The people had missed the point of the commandments and the sacrifices made at the temple. God did not desire that the people would violate His instructions and make up with Him by the blood and burning flesh of animals. He has no need of the sacrifices, His desire was that they would trust Him enough to obey His commandments, statutes, and instructions, that they would be blessed and prosper. He provided the sacrifices as a precaution in case they missed the mark, so that they had a way to get back in line with God.

- Vs. 6-7
  "*Is* this not the fast that I have chosen: To loose the bonds of wickedness, To undo the heavy burdens, To let the oppressed go free and that you break every yoke? Is it not to share your bread with the hungry, And that you bring to your house the poor who are cast out; When you see the naked, that you cover him, And not hide yourself from your own flesh?"

  - Shouldn't we instead be fasting and praying that God would bring justice and righteousness and blessing?

  - Shouldn't we use our time of fasting to do things such as giving our food (which we are fasting from) to the hungry who cannot afford food? Isn't this the righteous and upright behavior that the LORD expects from those who carry His name (CHRISTians)?

"Then your light shall break forth like the morning, your healing shall spring forth speedily, and your righteousness shall go before you; the glory of the Lord shall be your rear guard. Then you shall call, and the Lord will answer; you shall cry, and He will say, 'Here I am.' "If you take away the yoke from your midst, the pointing of the finger, and speaking wickedness, If you extend your soul to the hungry and satisfy the afflicted soul, then your light shall dawn in the darkness, and your darkness shall be as the noonday. The Lord will guide you continually, and satisfy your soul in drought, and strengthen your bones; you shall be like a watered garden, and like a spring of water, whose waters do not fail. Those from among you shall build the old waste places; You shall raise up the foundations of many generations; and you shall be called the Repairer of the Breach, The Restorer of Streets to Dwell In." (Isaiah 58:8-12)

These are the results of fasting in righteousness, the fast of the LORD.

Truly the LORD does desire that His saints would fast, but not that they would fast to show their sorrow and repentance, but rather that we would walk in obedience and fast that He might hear our cries for justice and blessing:

"But the people took of the plunder, sheep and oxen, the best of the things which should have been utterly destroyed, to sacrifice to the LORD your God in Gilgal." So Samuel said: "Has the LORD *as great* delight in burnt offerings and sacrifices, as in obeying the voice of the LORD? Behold, to obey is better than sacrifice, *and* to heed than the fat of rams. For rebellion *is as* the sin of witchcraft, and stubbornness *is as* iniquity and idolatry. Because you have rejected the word of the LORD He also has rejected you from *being* king." (1 Samuel 15:21-23)

Jesus gives us some insight as to how to conduct ourselves during a fast:

"Moreover, when you fast, do not be like the hypocrites, with a sad countenance. For they disfigure their faces that they may appear to men to be fasting. Assuredly, I say to you, they have their reward. But you, when you fast, anoint your head and wash your face, so that you do not appear to men to be fasting, but to your Father who *is* in the secret *place;* and your Father who sees in secret will reward you openly. "Do not lay up for yourselves treasures on earth, where moth and rust destroy and where thieves break in and steal; but lay up for yourselves treasures in heaven, where neither moth nor rust destroys and where thieves do not break in and steal. For where your treasure is, there your heart will be also." (Matthew 6:16-21)

CHAPTER 7

Chapter 7.
Consecration

"Consecrate yourselves therefore, and be holy, for I am the Lord your God. And you shall keep My statutes, and perform them: I am the Lord who sanctifies you."
(Leviticus 20:7-8)

Consecrate" is the Hebrew word, "Qadash", which means to be, to cause to be, make pronounce, or observe as holy (set apart / not for common usage).

"Also Moses took the anointing oil, and anointed the tabernacle and all that *was* in it, and consecrated them. He sprinkled some of it on the altar seven times, anointed the altar and all its utensils, and the laver and its base, to consecrate them. And he poured some of the anointing oil on Aaron's head and anointed him, to consecrate him." (Leviticus 8:10-12)

In this same manner God called for all priests to be consecrated for service to God, every priest must be consecrated!!! This is significant considering that we, the Church, are now also the priesthood of God:

"But you *are* a chosen generation, a royal priesthood, a holy nation, His own special people, that you may proclaim the praises of Him who called you out of darkness into His marvelous light" (1 Peter 2:9)

God calls for his people to actively consecrate themselves! The Scriptures definitely illustrate that there is power from God associated with the consecration of oneself.

> "And when they had come to the multitude, a man came to Him, kneeling down to Him and saying, "Lord, have mercy on my son, for he is an epileptic and suffers severely; for he often falls into the fire and often into the water. So I brought him to Your disciples, but they could not cure him." Then Jesus answered and said, "O faithless and perverse generation, how long shall I be with you? How long shall I bear with you? Bring him here to Me." And Jesus rebuked the demon, and it came out of him; and the child was cured from that very hour. Then the disciples came to Jesus privately and said, "Why could we not cast it out?" So Jesus said to them, "Because of your unbelief; for assuredly, I say to you, if you have faith as a mustard seed, you will say to this mountain, 'Move from here to there,' and it will move; and nothing will be impossible for you. However, this kind does not go out except by prayer and fasting." (Matthew 17:14-21)

Prayer and fasting are the two most normative ways a person may consecrate (set themselves apart unto God) himself.

Jesus Himself did not even begin his ministry until he first went away into the wilderness (separated Himself) and consecrated Himself to the Lord by fasting and prayer

Also observe, when Jesus had consecrate himself to the Lord forty days and forty nights, then the tempter came to him, but Jesus, though His flesh was made weak through fasting, His spirit was strong through prayer and **internal dedication** to God, and so he soundly defeated every temptation of the enemy by simply trusting in, and quoting, the written Word.

Make no mistake about it, when you consecrate yourself to the Lord by fasting and prayer, you are humbling yourself, making yourself low in acknowledgement that God is higher (mightier, wiser, of greater value) than you. Thusly, to humble oneself through consecration is worship.

When a person humbles himself before the Lord, he exalts God in His inward man, and though he may appear to men to be lowered, the scripture says that God Himself will exalt (lift up make higher, mightier, wiser, more valuable) such a person:

"Humble yourselves in the sight of the Lord, and He will lift you up." (James 4:10)

If we, as a people, desire to experience God in a mightier way, we must prepare ourselves for the presence of God lest his very glory be the death of us.

And Joshua said to the people, "Sanctify yourselves, for tomorrow the LORD will do wonders among you." (Joshua 3:5)

The power of God is too much for the carnal man to withstand, we must become more spiritual, we must draw closer to God with our inner man before we can stand to be blessed by His weighty presence (glory). If we attempt to get closer to him (by way of consecration) we can be assured that He will bring His Self closer to us.

"Therefore submit to God. Resist the devil and he will flee from you. Draw near to God and He will draw near to you. Cleanse *your* hands, *you* sinners; and purify *your* hearts, *you* double-minded." (James 4:7-8)

James was also making it quite clear that part of drawing closer to God was to separate oneself from sin and wickedness, "Cleanse your hands, you sinners; and purify your hearts, you double-minded."

Whereas consecrating yourself to God through fasting and prayer is a mighty way to secure your victory over the schemes and devices of the devil, if we are in sin, if we harbor sin or make allowance for it, we negate our righteousness and cancel our own victory, a person who is in sin cannot take authority over the author of sin.

"Get up, sanctify the people, and say, 'Sanctify yourselves for tomorrow, because thus says the LORD God of Israel:

"*There is* an accursed thing in your midst, O Israel; you cannot stand before your enemies until you take away the accursed thing from among you." (Joshua 7:13)

It is pointless to fast and pray while willfully remaining in sin, observe the Word of the LORD revealed through the prophet Isaiah:

“Behold, the LORD's hand is not shortened, that it cannot save; nor His ear heavy, yhat it cannot hear. But your iniquities have separated you from your God; and your sins have hidden *His* face from you, so that He will not hear.” (Isaiah 59:1-2)

When done correctly, with repentance, and with a true heart of devotion to God, consecration actually makes a person holy to God. The person who is consecrated to God has a special connection to God, you actually open your spirit to hear from his Spirit, and receive supernatural strength from God. Let us look to Sampson, how did he get his strength?

“Again the children of Israel did evil in the sight of the LORD, and the LORD delivered them into the hand of the Philistines for forty years. Now there was a certain man from Zorah, of the family of the Danites, whose name *was* Manoah; and his wife *was* barren and had no children. And the Angel of the LORD appeared to the woman and said to her, "Indeed now, you are barren and have borne no children, but you shall conceive and bear a son. Now therefore, please be careful not to drink wine or *similar* drink, and not to eat anything unclean. For behold, you shall conceive and bear a son. And no razor shall come upon his head, for the child shall be a Nazirite to God from the womb; and he shall begin to deliver Israel out of the hand of the Philistines." (Judges 13:1-5)

"So the woman bore a son and called his name Samson; and the child grew, and the LORD blessed him. And the Spirit of the LORD began to move upon him at Mahaneh Dan between Zorah and Eshtaol." (Judges 13:24-25)

Even in the womb, the consecrated child Samson had the Spirit of the Lord moving upon him.

If you need a word from the Lord, Moses has set the example, he was on the mountain of the Lord, consecrated through fasting and prayer for forty days and forty nights when he was blessed to receive the Ten Commandments, carved in stone by the very finger of God!

After Moses came down from the mountain and saw the debauchery of the children of Israel, how they had already returned to worshiping idols, he cast down the tablets of stone and broke them.

But God was gracious enough to give the Ten Commandments a second time, this time again Moses was consecrated to the Lord forty days and forty nights with fasting and prayer to deliver the Word of God:

“Then the LORD said to Moses, "Write these words, for according to the tenor of these words I have made a covenant with you and with Israel." So he was there with the LORD forty days and forty nights; he neither ate bread nor drank water. And He wrote on the tablets the words of the covenant, the Ten Commandments. Now it was so, when Moses came down from Mount Sinai (and the two tablets of the Testimony *were* in Moses' hand when he came down from the mountain), that Moses did not know that the skin of his face shone while he talked with Him. So when Aaron and all the children of Israel saw Moses, behold, the skin of his face shone, and they were afraid to come near him.” (Exodus 34:27-30)

Let it be noted, that Jesus, who is our example, regularly consecrated himself.

> "So He Himself often withdrew into the wilderness and prayed.” (Luke 5:16)

Not only did Jesus set the example, but He also gave instruction that we should, from time to time, separate ourselves to devote our entire attention to Him in prayer.

“But you, when you pray, go into your room, and when you have shut your door, pray to your Father who *is* in the secret *place;* and your Father who sees in secret will reward you openly.” (Matthew 6:6)

SECTION 3

CHAPTER 8

Chapter 8.
Evangelism

"And he said unto them, Go ye into all the world, and preach the gospel to every creature." (Mark 16:15)

Empowered For The Work

"But you shall receive power when the Holy Spirit has come upon you; and you shall be witnesses to Me in Jerusalem, and in all Judea and Samaria, and to the end of the earth." (Acts 1:8)

"Power" is the Greek word, "dunamis", which means force, miraculous ability, dynamic strength, (dynamite power).

"Witnesses" is the Greek word, "martus", which means a martyr, one who bears record, a witness.

- Martyr = **1** - a person who voluntarily suffers death as the penalty of witnessing to and refusing to renounce a religion **2** - a person who sacrifices something of great value and especially life itself for the sake of principle

Acts 1:8 says that when we receive the Holy Spirit we also receive the miraculous, God-given, and dynamic ability sacrifice any and every thing for the cause of Christ and the birthing of others into His Kingdom! This ministry which is incumbent upon us from the moment of our regeneration is to be carried out in every place beginning in Jerusalem (your immediate city / area), Judea (the surrounding areas), and to the end of the earth (everywhere in the world).

You reach your Jerusalem through the outreach ministries of the local assembly. Every Christian should have experience in the simple measures of one to one witnessing, door to door outreach, and relationship evangelism.

You reach your Judea and Samaria through expansive activities, church planting, church fellowship, and cooperation with existing ministries.

You reach to the end of the earth through international missions, and, due to the advent of streaming technologies, we now can reach the world through live streaming on a multitude of platforms.

God has empowered His saints, by the Holy Spirit, to reach both near and far with the glorious gospel of Jesus Christ. You have been empowered to share the truth of Christ and His soon coming Kingdom with both your family and the most random of strangers!

Called For The Work

"And Jesus came and spoke to them, saying, "All authority has been given to Me in heaven and on earth. Go therefore and make disciples of all the nations, baptizing them in the name of the Father and of the Son and of the Holy Spirit, teaching them to observe all things that I have commanded you; and lo, I am with you always, *even* to the end of the age. Amen." (Matthew 28:18-20)

Jesus is, Himself, the central focus and the authorizing figure of the Great Commission. Notice that He said, "All authority has been given to Me… Go therefore…". The reason that the disciples are to go is because all authority has been given to Jesus. It not usually noticed that the commission is not the central point of this passage, the chief thought is that Jesus has ALL authority and is now, by that authority, sending His disciples into the world to act on His authority.

Jesus continues, "… and make disciples of all the nations…". "Make disciples" is the Greek word, "matheteuo", meaning to teach, to make students.

Evangelism involves the element of teaching (pointing out truth). Interesting enough, the word "Torah", most often translated as "law", is actually more accurately translated as "instruction", "doctrine", or "teaching". Further study reveals that Torah is understood as "that which is pointed out". Christ has called for His followers to go forth and point out that the way to God is only through the Messiah, Jesus Christ.

Jesus continued, "... baptizing them in the name...". The result should be that souls, having received the gospel, and placing their trust in Christ, should then submit to His authority through water baptism in the name of He who has the authority.

We are not bearing witness to the truth of this gospel aimlessly, but with a goal of conversion in mind. Jesus has not called the Church to preach just to be preaching, but rather so that souls might properly respond to His sacrifice and victory over death by submitting to His authority and, thereby, themselves receiving victory over death through the in-filling of God's Holy Spirit.

"And He said to them, "Go into all the world and preach the gospel to every creature. He who believes and is baptized will be saved; but he who does not believe will be condemned. And these signs will follow those who believe: In My name they will cast out demons; they will speak with new tongues; they will take up serpents; and if they drink anything deadly, it will by no means hurt them; they will lay hands on the sick, and they will recover." (Mark 16:15-18)

Firstly, note that Jesus did not say "wait for them to come to church, and preach to them". He said GO!

"Go" means to **move** out of or away from a place expressed or implied.

One of the things the unproductive servant in the parable of the talents was rebuked for was being slothful (lazy). We must understand that the great commission is a call to action, Jesus said "go", we must be actively pursuing opportunities to share the gospel on a daily basis and we must be participants in mission, whether through being participants, or supporters (finances and prayer).

Jesus continued, "...and preach the gospel..."

"Preach" is the Greek word, "kerusso", meaning to proclaim, to publish, to make known.

Preaching, scripturally speaking, is not what we think it is. When we think of preaching, we think of a pastor in a pulpit robe, standing behind a podium on a platform inside of a church building, taking a text, expounding on it, and probably getting excited, sweating, yelling, whooping, tuning up, and finally closing (maybe three or four times). Scripturally speaking, this activity of speaking to mostly the saints, generally stirring their faith and encouraging their obedient actions toward God, is what would be called exhortation.

Scriptural preaching is simply the proclaiming or declaration of the gospel of Jesus Christ, in all of its many iterations. What is generally meant is what we normally think of as "witnessing". One on one interactions with the purpose of bringing a soul to Christ. Biblical preaching often takes place on the phone, in the line of the grocery store, on the bus, at a coffee shop, or anywhere where people can talk. In short, every Christian is called to preach. You are a preacher!

This means that the great commission is simply the call for you to tell somebody about Jesus!

Jesus continued, “He who believes and is baptized will be saved”

“Believes” is the Greek word, “pisteuo”, meaning to have faith. This is the Greek version of the Hebrew word “emunah”, meaning to trust confidently, to be firm, to have an unshakeable trust, hence, faith.

To paraphrase the, “He who has **faith** and acts on it (is baptized) shall receive the Promise of salvation”.

Faith without works is dead, meaning void, empty, powerless, fruitless, and pointless. Faith, which is a rock solid confident trust, must be expressed through corresponding action. If a person says they trust, but doesn’t act trustingly, their actions betray their true condition of doubt. Hence, Jesus prescribes the appropriate corresponding action for one who professes to have faith to be saved, “he who believes and is baptized shall be saved”. This is stating that a person who receives the gospel, trusts in Christ, and is willing to do whatever is required by God (this is the mindset which is called repentance), inclusive of submitting to water baptism, will, in fact, receive the baptism of the Holy Spirit (salvation).

Thusly we see that Christian baptism is indispensable to the Christian faith in general and to salvation specifically.

Finally Jesus continues, "And these signs will follow those who believe...". We must EXPECT supernatural manifestations whenever we declare the good news about Jesus Christ! The message of the free gift of salvation through Jesus Christ is intended to be accompanied by the demonstration of God's power. Healings, deliverance from demons, even the raising of the dead should be expected where the truth of Christ is declare. I personally bear witness to the fact that God is still doing miracles today! May all of God's people have enough confidence in God to call for miracles and expect them to manifest!

Equipped For The Work

Simple principles of Gospel witnessing

1. Everyone is born a sinner, being born without the Spirit of Holiness (Holy Ghost).

2. A perfectly righteous God must bring judgment against **all** sin.

3. God loves you so much that He took on a human body in order to receive the judgment for your sins in your place.

4. God requires that you acknowledge His sacrifice, trust that it is sufficient to remove your sins, and willingly become obedient to Him.

5. Upon your submission to Him, He will change your status from "sinner" to "saint" (holy one) by putting His Spirit of Holiness in you. This is the meaning of being "born again".

This is more than a religious experience. It is an entrance into the community of God (the Kingdom of Heaven).

Wisdom For The Work

"The fruit of the righteous *is a* tree of life, And he who wins souls *is* wise." (Proverbs 11:30)

"Those who are wise shall shine Like the brightness of the firmament, And those who turn many to righteousness Like the stars forever and ever." (Daniel 12:3)

This term, "Those who are wise shall shine", naturally brings one to the question, who are the wise?

"Behold, I send you out as sheep in the midst of wolves. Therefore be wise as serpents and harmless as doves." (Matthew 10:16)

The followers of Christ are called to be wise. There are many definitions for wisdom, but one of the simplest is that wisdom is "God's way". If a person follows God's way, that person will be acting and living in wisdom. Another definition is that wisdom is insight. When a person is living in tune with the Spirit of God, they will have access to divine insight and guidance that empowers them to succeed. Living in wisdom by following the Spirit of God will lead a person into soul winning because God will put you in the right place at the right time and give you the right words at the right moment. Soul winning doesn't require any self-confidence at all, it simply requires that a person live in full submission to the leading of the Holy Spirit.

The book of Daniel said that the wise shall, "shine like the brightness of the firmament (stars in the sky)"

"The Son of Man will send out His angels, and they will gather out of His kingdom all things that offend, and those who practice lawlessness, and will cast them into the furnace of fire. There will be wailing and gnashing of teeth. Then the righteous will **shine** forth as the sun in the kingdom of their Father. He who has ears to hear, let him hear! (Matthew 13:41-43)

Wisdom is related to righteousness, the wise shall shine like stars (the brightness of the firmament), and the righteous shall shine like the sun. The wisdom of following God faithfully results in the life of righteousness, which causes a person to be a light in the darkness, like John the Baptist, a bright and shinning light (see John 5:33-35).

“Indeed He says, 'It is too small a thing that You should be My Servant To raise up the tribes of Jacob, And to restore the preserved ones of Israel; I will also give You as a **light** to the Gentiles, That You should be My salvation to the ends of the earth.'" (Isaiah 49:6)

In Acts 13:47 Paul quotes this very verse and applies it to the Church (Body of Christ), showing that God has determined for **US** to be a light to the nations (Gentiles/the world).

"You are the light of the world. A city that is set on a hill cannot be hidden. Nor do they light a lamp and put it under a basket, but on a lampstand, and it gives light to all *who are* in the house. Let your light so shine before men, that they may see your good works and glorify your Father in heaven.” (Matthew 5:14-16)

We share in the glory of our King when we work to expand His reign! “For what *is* our hope, or joy, or crown of rejoicing? *Is it* not even you in the presence of our Lord Jesus Christ at His coming? For you are our glory and joy.” (1 Thessalonians 2:19-20)

CHAPTER 9

Chapter 9.
Prophetic Ministry

"And it shall come to pass afterward
That I will pour out My Spirit on all flesh;
Your sons and your daughters shall prophesy,
Your old men shall dream dreams,
Your young men shall see visions."
(Joel 2:28)

The Spirit of Prophecy

"And I fell at his feet to worship him. But he said to me, "See *that you do* not *do that!* I am your fellow servant, and of your brethren who have the testimony of Jesus. Worship God! **For the testimony of Jesus is the spirit of prophecy**." (Revelation 19:10)

Do you have the testimony of Jesus? Do you acknowledge that He is, in fact, the Christ, the Son of the living God? Are you filled with His Spirit? If your answer is "yes", you have the testimony of Jesus, and, therefore, the Spirit of prophecy.

Prophecy is the inspired expression of divine revelation. Inspired means "God breathed" (Gk. "theopneustos"). This means prophecy cannot come from man's spirit, but only from God's Spirit!

Many people think that prophecy means telling the future, but in reality telling the future is only a small aspect of prophecy. Prophets in the Old Testament were primarily charged with calling God's people to repent, return to the LORD, and return to obeying His commandments and instructions. When the people persisted in their rebellion against the Almighty, then the prophets would be sent to tell them of the ensuing punishment. For the most part prophets came to forthtell (speak out) for God, when they had to foretell (tell the future) it was generally a very negative thing. With this in mind, be aware that, if you have received the baptism of the Holy Spirit, God has put the same Holy Spirit in you that was upon the prophets of old, and God wants to reveal His will to you, He wants you to operate in the prophetic!

God has numerous ways of sending prophetic expressions:

- **Prophetic dreams**. Seeing in a different dimension while asleep.

"For God may speak in one way, or in another, yet man does not perceive it. In a dream, in a vision of the night, when deep sleep falls upon men, while slumbering on their beds, Then He opens the ears of men, and seals their instruction. (Job 33:14-16)

God often speaks to us in our dreams, God expresses His will through visions in the night, bypassing the conscious mind and sealing His instructions in the mind.

- **Open vision**. Being immersed in seeing in a different dimension while awake.

“I was in the Spirit on the Lord's Day, and I heard behind me a loud voice, as of a trumpet, saying, "I am the Alpha and the Omega, the First and the Last," and, "What you see, write in a book and send it to the seven churches which are in Asia: to Ephesus, to Smyrna, to Pergamos, to Thyatira, to Sardis, to Philadelphia, and to Laodicea.“ Then I turned to see the voice that spoke with me. And having turned I saw seven golden lampstands, and in the midst of the seven lampstands One like the Son of Man, clothed with a garment down to the feet and girded about the chest with a golden band.” (Revelation 1:10-13)

Notice John said he was “in the Spirit” on the Lord’s Day. It is believed that John was in the midst of worship when he found himself moved from simply experiencing the natural realm to experiencing the spiritual dimension (in the Spirit). Everything that comes afterward in the book of the Revelation is what John both saw and heard in this immersive spiritual experience.

- **Interdimensional vision**. Seeing in two dimensions simultaneously.

“And when the servant of the man of God arose early and went out, there was an army, surrounding the city with horses and chariots. And his servant said to him, "Alas, my master! What shall we do?" So he answered, "Do not fear, for those who are with us are more than those who are with them." And Elisha prayed, and said, "Lord, I pray, open his eyes that he may see." Then the Lord opened the eyes of the young man, and he saw. And behold, the mountain was full of horses and chariots of fire all around Elisha.” (2 Kings 6:15-18)

The difference between John’s experience and that of Elisha’s servant is that John no longer experienced or saw the island of Patmos while having his vision of the revelation, but Elisha’s servant didn’t have his surroundings disappear, but instead, in addition to what he saw in the natural dimension, hills and men, he also saw the spiritual reality that overlapped it, thusly seeing the angels that surrounded them, which were invisible to all but Elisha and his servant.

This type of vision is seeing in both the natural and the spiritual dimensions simultaneously. I have experienced this many times. I have seen words and objects floating above people’s heads.

- **Audible voice of the LORD**. Hearing God's voice in your physical ear.

"And the Lord came, and stood, and called as at other times, Samuel, Samuel. Then Samuel answered, Speak; for thy servant heareth." (1 Samuel 3:10)

This is more rare than the others, but it does still happen. God can speak to you so that you hear Him audibly with your physical ears. This experience was so evidently external to Samuel that he actually thought it was Eli calling him!

- **Still small voice** (inward whisper). Hearing God's voice in your spiritual ear (hearing in your spirit).

"Then He said, "Go out, and stand on the mountain before the Lord." And behold, the Lord passed by, and a great and strong wind tore into the mountains and broke the rocks in pieces before the Lord, but the Lord was not in the wind; and after the wind an earthquake, but the Lord was not in the earthquake; and after the earthquake a fire, but the Lord was not in the fire; and after the fire a still small voice. So it was, when Elijah heard it, that he wrapped his face in his mantle and went out and stood in the entrance of the cave. Suddenly a voice came to him, and said, "What are you doing here, Elijah?" (1 Kings 19:11-13)

God speaks to us often through His Holy Spirit within us.

This is the still small voice, the voice of God speaking to you from the inside. It is so distinctly not you that you need not question if it was God or not. God's Spirit will speak within your spirit and give you wisdom beyond your experience, knowledge beyond your learning, and peace beyond your understanding!

- **Discernment** (supernatural knowing). Sensing or knowing supernaturally in your spirit without the aid of external information.

"Now the king of Syria was making war against Israel; and he consulted with his servants, saying, "My camp will be in such and such a place." And the man of God sent to the king of Israel, saying, "Beware that you do not pass this place, for the Syrians are coming down there." Then the king of Israel sent someone to the place of which the man of God had told him. Thus he warned him, and he was watchful there, not just once or twice." (2 Kings 6:8-10)

Spiritual discernment is a supernatural knowing. It is not, as many people attempt to claim they are using it, a suspicion of others. To know is to possess knowledge. Spiritual discernment is the possession of knowledge concerning a person, place, thing, or situation that was not gained through natural means.

- **Prophetic oracles**. Prophesy spoken by others (including sermons)

"...Hear me, O Judah and you inhabitants of Jerusalem: Believe in the Lord your God, and you shall be established; believe His prophets, and you shall prosper." (2 Chronicles 20:20)

God doesn't only speak to you for you, He also speaks to others for your life. Primarily through your pastor and local spiritual leaders, however, He also from time to time may use others outside of your normal circle to speak the prophetic into your life.

God speaks through group prophesy, personal prophesy, and even through the individualized revelations that are gained through the publically preached word.

Everyone who has received the Holy Spirit has the testimony of Jesus Christ (salvific faith in His gospel), and, therefore, has access to all of these means of prophetic revelation and more!

Importance of the prophetic

Kingdom living is operating by prophetic insight. We are not intended to live by natural observance, cultural norms, or even common sense. The Christian is intended and expected to be prophetic, being led by the Spirit of God in their daily life. There is nothing more beneficial to any individuals life than the Word of the LORD.

“Your word *is* a lamp to my feet a light to my path. (Psalm 119:105)

Every Kingdom Citizen (Christian) must follow the path set forth by the Word of the LORD. The prophetic lifestyle of the Kingdom dweller is revealed in the fact that the just shall live by faith (Habakkuk 2:2 / Romans 1:17):

“So then faith *comes* by hearing, and hearing by the word of God.” (Romans 10:17)

“Word”, in Romans 10:17, is the Greek word, “rhema”, which means utterance, thing said (indicating the action of the utterance), a message.

A “logos” is literally a word, the sound made or combination of symbols seen, when letters are combined, but the “rhema” is the message intended by the words.

God’s rhema Word (prophetic revelation) is a lamp to our feet and a light to our path (Psalm 119:105)! The Word of God, both written in the Bible, and prophetic rhema Word, causes us to see ourselves as we truly are. It reveals God’s standard of perfect righteousness and, thereby, reveals our lack of perfect righteousness. The Word of the LORD reveals my current standing. Thy word is a lamp to my feet.

The Word of the LORD also reveals God’s way, God’s path that He desires me to take. This is the way that leads to my ultimate perfection in Christ. Only God’s Word illuminates the road that I should take. Thy word is a light to my path.

Levels of function in prophetic ministry

The Spirit of prophecy

This is the general level of prophecy available to every Spirit-filled believer. Every Spirit-filled Christian can and should yield to the Spirit of prophecy and speak the Word (rhema) of the LORD.

"...the testimony of Jesus is the spirit of prophecy." (Revelation 19:10)

The gift of prophecy

This person is particularly strong in the flow of the Spirit of prophecy and functions in it more often than the average believer.

A person who flows in the gift of prophesy may, and often does, operate primarily in the prophetic utterance giftings of 1 Corinthians 12:8-10, which are the word of wisdom, word of knowledge, prophecy, discerning of spirits, tongues, and interpretation of tongues.

There are many travelling exhorters ("evangelists") that have the gift of prophecy, and, as such, flow mightily in the word of knowledge, and/or discerning of spirits, and thereby they erroneously claim for themselves the office of the prophet.

The office of the prophet

Prophecy is the primary function and purpose of the prophet's life. Speaking forth the rhema word is the reason why the prophet lives and breathes. Prophet are sensitive to the heart of God, they are called to proclaim the mind of God to society, priests, kings, and average people alike.

Prophets generally have a deep burning passion to see God's people living faithfully in the righteousness of God through Jesus Christ, and are usually irate when corruption is present in the Church.

The office of the prophet is a very significant one, and because of the important role they play in the Kingdom, that of being course correctors, they tend to live under constant demonic attack. Real prophets, however, are born for the task at hand and are able to withstand the onslaught of infernal warfare to the glory of God.

It must be noted that no seminar, class, or rite of ordination can make you into a prophet. Either you were born a prophet or you will never be one. God distributes the gifts in His Church according to His own prerogatives.

Receiving the prophetic

"Do not quench the Spirit. Do not despise prophecies. Test all things; hold fast what is good."
(1 Thessalonians 5:19-21)

First note that it says, "do not quench the Spirit". The word quench means to extinguish, to put out. The Spirit of God desires to speak in the assembly of the saints. God desires to work His miracles, signs, and wonders in, through, for, and by the saints. It is a horrendous travesty for the very saints that He wants to bless with His presence and Word to outlaw the moving of His Spirit through prophecy in the Church. Do not attempt to handcuff God.

Secondly note that it says, "do not despise prophecies". There are some houses of worship that accept divine healing and speaking in tongues, but forbid anyone from prophesying. This simply makes no sense. The Kingdom of Heaven is not a smorgasbord where you can pick and choose the manifestations of the Spirit that you want and outlaw the others! Let God have His way. Do not despise prophecies.

Then, finally it says, "test all things" and "hold fast what is good".

Everything is to be tested. No “blind faith” here. God does not desire mindless zombies, He wants thinking Kingdom Citizens who consider His Word in order that they might obey it! Of course there are false prophets, of course there are false prophecies, this only proves the existence of the authentic even more. Nobody counterfeits eight dollar bills. Why? Because everyone knows there is no such thing, so no store or bank would accept them for payment. You only counterfeit something that is real!

Since there will be fakes and phonies, God prescribes, not that the Church throw out all prophecy and prophets, but rather that we learn to discern between what is real from Him and when we are witnessing “flesh on parade”.

“Beloved, do not believe every spirit, but test the spirits, whether they are of God; because many false prophets have gone out into the world.” (1 John 4:1)

The two primary ways to test prophecy is by the scripture and by actual fulfillments.

“And the word of the Lord came to Isaiah, saying, "Go and tell Hezekiah, 'Thus says the Lord, the God of David your father: "I have heard your prayer, I have seen your tears; surely I will add to your days fifteen years. I will deliver you and this city from the hand of the king of Assyria, and I will defend this city."' And this is the sign to you from the Lord, that the Lord will do this thing which He has spoken: Behold, I will bring the shadow on the sundial, which has gone down with the sun on the sundial of Ahaz, ten degrees backward." So the sun returned ten degrees on the dial by which it had gone down. (Isaiah 38:4-8)

Here God sent a word of the future, with a contemporary sign in order to confirm the Word to Hezekiah. Because it would be impossible to judge whether or not a person will live another fifteen years from the perspective of the present, God sent a sign that could be both observed and judged in the present, the shadow on the sundial moving ten degrees backward, in order to confirm (for judgment/testing) the prophetic promise concerning the future of Hezekiah.

"But the prophet who presumes to speak a word in My name, which I have not commanded him to speak, or who speaks in the name of other gods, that prophet shall die.' And if you say in your heart, 'How shall we know the word which the Lord has not spoken?' — when a prophet speaks in the name of the Lord, if the thing does not happen or come to pass, that is the thing which the Lord has not spoken; the prophet has spoken it presumptuously; you shall not be afraid of him." (Deuteronomy 18:20-22)

The main danger of the prophetic is when unproven people give an unproven Word that goes untested by scripture and fulfillment, but is embraced by people with itching ears who are duped thereby. A person who stands as a prophet, but their word is untested, become a danger to the entire community of Christ.

The Prophetic Life

"For if you live according to the flesh you will die; but if by the Spirit you put to death the deeds of the body, you will live. For as many as are led by the Spirit of God, these are sons of God. (Romans 8:13-14)

Living according to the flesh is following the lead of your selfish/self-centered thinking. The Flesh/Self is the carnal/inward focused mindset that is anchored to this temporal world.

A mindset is a fixed mental attitude or disposition that predetermines a person's responses to and interpretations of situations.

The flesh (self-worship) is put to death when we instead obey the leading of God's Holy Spirit.

Being led by (following/obeying) the Holy Spirit is the only way to access eternal life (connection to God)!

Rebellion/Failure to comply is the chief destroyer of connection/relationship with God.

"But your iniquities have separated you from your God; and your sins have hidden His face from you, so that He will not hear." (Isaiah 59:2)

This is the only way to access eternal life (connection to God). Those who God will count as His own children (saved) will be those who, not only receive the Holy Spirit, but follow Him in obedience.

“I say then: Walk in the Spirit, and you shall not fulfill the lust of the flesh.” (Galatians 5:16)

Walking in the Spirit is simply following the lead of the Holy Spirit. “...the testimony of Jesus is the spirit of prophecy” (Revelation 19:10), everyone who has the Holy Spirit has the testimony of Jesus, and, therefore, the spirit of prophecy.

“Then Moses said to him, "Are you zealous for my sake? Oh, that all the LORD's people were prophets *and* that the LORD would put His Spirit upon them!" (Numbers 11:29)

Moses desired that ALL of God’s people would have the Holy Spirit upon them and be able to prophesy, this is exactly what is accomplished in Christ.

Functioning in the Spirit of Prophecy

“After that you shall come to the hill of God where the Philistine garrison *is.* And it will happen, when you have come there to the city, that you will meet a group of prophets coming down from the high place with a stringed instrument, a tambourine, a flute, and a harp before them; and they will be prophesying. Then the Spirit of the LORD will come upon you, and you will prophesy with them and be turned into another man. (1 Samuel 10:5-6)

The anointing to prophesy is increased in the presence of prophets and prophetic people. This is one of the many reasons that God has created the holy assembly (the Church), so that we might be strengthened by one-another. The anointing is transferrable. When you are around people who flow in the prophetic, your prophetic anointing is stirred within you.

The anointing to prophesy is increased by spiritual music.

“And Elisha said, "*As* the LORD of hosts lives, before whom I stand, surely were it not that I regard the presence of Jehoshaphat king of Judah, I would not look at you, nor see you. But now bring me a musician." Then it happened, when the musician played, that the hand of the LORD came upon him. And he said, "Thus says the LORD: 'Make this valley full of ditches.'” (2 Kings 3:14-16)

The hand of the LORD came upon the prophet, the Holy Spirit was stirred in/upon the prophet when the musician began to play. Music is a tool that can help us to “tune in” to the Spirit and the move of God!

Music was invented by God and has incredible spiritual effects in every situation. We see in 1 Samuel 16:14-23 that a distressing spirit was upon King Saul, and when David played skillfully upon the harp, that distressing spirit would depart from Saul, and he would be well. This should cause you to be aware (beware) of what manner of music you are allowing to enter your soul through the ear gate! Just as godly and holy music calls forth and stirs us the Holy Spirit, so does evil and profane music call forth and stir up evil and unclean spirits.

The prophet told Saul that you will prophesy.

"Prophesy" is the Hebrew word, "naba", which means to prophesy, to flow, to spring, to bubble up. This indicates inspired (bubbling up) speech. The potent Word of the LORD that He causes to bubble up inside of you like a soda pop that has been violently shaken. This Word must come out! This internal pressure that compels the inspired to speak forth the prophecy is what Jeremiah was eluding to when he said, "Then I said, "I will not make mention of Him,

Nor speak anymore in His name." But His word was in my heart like a burning fire shut up in my bones; I was weary of holding it back, and I could not." (Jeremiah 20:9)

God can cause His Word to bubble up from inside of you like hot lava! Like fire shut up in your bones, it must be released.

Speaking of prophecy in another place the scripture says: "The earth shook, the heavens also dropped at the presence of God: even Sinai itself was moved at the presence of God, the God of Israel." (Psalm 68:8)

Drop is the Hebrew word, "Nataph", which means to drop, to drip, to distil, to discourse, (figuratively) to speak by inspiration (prophesy).

God can cause heavenly revelation to drop upon you like dew or rain, and thereby give you inspired speech (prophecy).

"Moreover the word of the Lord came unto me, saying,

Son of man, set thy face toward the south, and drop thy word toward the south, and prophesy against the forest of the south field" (Ezekiel 20:45-46)

Ezekiel is told to drop (nataph) and to prophesy (nabi). Here we see that one person in one situation can bring forth the prophetic word in multiple ways, Ezekiel is instructed to speak both the Word that drops from heaven, as well as the Word that bubbles up inside of him!

"Unto me men gave ear, and waited, and kept silence at my counsel. After my words they spake not again; and my speech dropped upon them. 23 And they waited for me as for the rain; and they opened their mouth wide as for the latter rain." (Job 29:21-23)

CHAPTER 10

Chapter 10.
Deliverance Ministry

"And when He had called His twelve disciples to Him, He gave them power over unclean spirits, to cast them out, and to heal all kinds of sickness and all kinds of disease."
(Matthew 10:1-2)

Possessed or demonized?

There are four different words in our Bible that are translated into English as "possessed":

1) **huparchonta** (hoop-ar'-khon-tah) things extant or in hand, i.e. property or possessions:

This word, translated as "possessed" appears only one time in the bible, in Acts 4:32, speaking of the unity of the saints and how they had all things in common, not supposing that anything which they owned (possessed) was their own, but instead sharing with the holy community of God (the Church).

2) **katecho** (kat-ekh'-o); from NT:2596 and NT:2192; to hold down (fast), in various applications (literally or figuratively)

This word, translated as "possessed" appears only one time in the bible, in 1 Corinthians 7:30, speaking of the end times, saying that those who buy things should not cleave to them as if possessions were more important than God.

3) **echo** (ekh'-o); including an alternate form **scheo** (skheh'-o); used in certain tenses only); a primary verb; to hold (used in very various applications, literally or figuratively, direct or remote; such as possessions; ability, continuity, relation, or condition):

This word, translated as "possessed" appears twice in the Bible, Acts 8:7 and Acts 16:16, both times speaking of someone being deeply entangled with, or held by, demons.

4) **daimonizomai** (dahee-mon-id'-zom-ahee); middle voice from NT:1142; to be exercised by a daemon:

This word, translated as "possessed" appears eleven times in the bible, in Matthew 4:24, Matthew 8:16, Matthew 8:28, Matthew 8:33, Matthew 9:32, Matthew 12:22, Mark 1:32, Mark 5:15, Mark 5:16, Mark 5:18, and Luke 8:36, and speaks each time of a person or people who have a demon (demons).

Daimonizomai should rightly be translated as “demonized” (Pigs in the Parlor chapter 1 page 9).

Daimonizomai has no indications of ownership. A demon **CANNOT** own a person.

“The earth is the LORD's, and the fulness thereof; the world, **and they that dwell therein**.” (Psalm 24:1)

“Exercise” is used in the verb form meaning “To use or apply”. A person who is “demonized” has a demon who is using their physical body to gratify itself. Demons living within a person will “put them through the paces”, exerting a strong influence over the life of the host in order to experience all manner of evil pleasure through the flesh of the host.

Further scholarship provides that it means to be vexed (tormented) by a demon. Having demons living within in never a pleasant experience. It may cause a person to feel and appear crazy. Many (but not all) people suffer the effects of being bipolar, schizophrenic, obsessive compulsive, multiple personality disorders, and other psychological problems due to the infestation of demons in the soul.

Possession is truly a misnomer, as demons cannot own people. Demons are like spiritual roaches.

Roaches don’t have houses. Houses have roaches.

Demons do not have people. People have demons.

Being demonized (having an evil spirit problem) does not mean you are a wicked person, but rather that your house (soul) is not clean, this problem needs to be solved. Demons must be exterminated.

They Shall Cast Out Devils!

"And he said unto them, Go ye into all the world, and preach the gospel to every creature. He that believeth and is baptized shall be saved; but he that believeth not shall be damned. And these signs shall follow them that believe; In my name shall they cast out devils; they shall speak with new tongues" (Mark 16:15-17)

The very first sign that Jesus listed of those who believe is that **THEY will cast out devils.**

Who are "THEY"?
"THEY" is a reference to those who believe (Gk. "pisteuo" meaning to have **faith**).
Are YOU of the faith of Jesus Christ? If your answer is "YES", then YOU are "THEY"! You are the one who is intended and expected by God to cast out devils! You don't have to call for the pastor or the priest, if you have the Holy Spirit, then you, in Jesus Christ, have authority over every devil and every demon!

How does it work?

“And these signs shall follow them that believe; **<u>In my name</u>** shall they cast out devils…”. The term, “in My name”, doesn’t mean for us to run around saying “in Jesus’ name” every time we do something, it means “by My authority”. We are called and empowered to expel demons by the authority of King Jesus Christ!

“And when he had called unto him his twelve disciples, he gave them power against unclean spirits, to cast them out, and to heal all manner of sickness and all manner of disease." (Matthew 10:1)

The text says Jesus gave them “power”, which is the Greek word “exousia”, meaning authority. In order for Jesus to give authority He must first have it, which He does.

“Then he called his twelve disciples together, and gave them power and authority over all devils, and to cure diseases.” (Luke 9:1)

“Behold, I give unto you power to tread on serpents and scorpions, and over all the power of the enemy: and nothing shall by any means hurt you.” (Luke 10:19)

Things To Remember

- It’s not your own might or power, but by the Spirit of God! (Zechariah 4:6)

- Keep Calm and Cast Out The Devil!
    - Don't let the devils draw you into their game of who can be louder or more demonstrative. Demons love to put on a show, but when a deliverance turns the church service into a circus environment it can cause more people to speculate than have faith. If a person is undergoing deliverance ministry and becomes loud or belligerent, it is often best to move that person to a private space and continue casting out devils as not to disrupt the entire service.

- Live a consecrated lifestyle, you never know when you will be called upon to take authority of the devils:

"And when they had come to the multitude, a man came to Him, kneeling down to Him and saying, "Lord, have mercy on my son, for he is an epileptic and suffers severely; for he often falls into the fire and often into the water. So I brought him to Your disciples, but they could not cure him." Then Jesus answered and said, "O faithless and perverse generation, how long shall I be with you? How long shall I bear with you? Bring him here to Me." And Jesus rebuked the demon, and it came out of him; and the child was cured from that very hour. Then the disciples came to Jesus privately and said, "Why could we not cast it out?" So Jesus said to them, "Because of your unbelief; for assuredly, I say to you, if you have faith as a mustard seed, you will say to this mountain, 'Move from here to there,' and it will move; and nothing will be impossible for you. However, this kind does not go out except by prayer and fasting." (Matthew 17:14-21)

Let us live prayer and fasting as a lifestyle, that we might be ever in tune with the Spirit of the LORD and always ready to minister in His power and authority.

God has called those who are full of His Spirit to be change agents in the world. We can no longer sit idly by and watch as the world goes to hell in a handbasket. We have the power to bring about change, we have the protocols of change. We have been called to shift into greater. We have been called to work the shift within ourselves. We have been called to SHIFT the World!

About the author

Apostle Mark A. Haywood serves as senior pastor of Greater Christ Temple Apostolic Church.

Born in Fort Wayne, Indiana to the union of the late Evg. Julia and Suffragan Bishop E.C. Haywood, Apostle Haywood was raised in the tradition of Apostolic holiness.

After laboring with the vision for more than three years, on June 14th 2005 Apostle Mark A. Haywood stepped out in faith, and with the blessing of his pastor, founded Christ Kingdom Church.

2013 brought Apostle Haywood back to where he started as he was called to return to his home church, Greater Christ Temple Apostolic Church, to be the successor to his natural father, Suffragan Bishop E.C. Haywood. On Sunday, January 26, 2014 Apostle Mark A. Haywood was installed as the senior pastor of Greater Christ Temple Apostolic Church, the oldest Pentecostal church in the city of Fort Wayne, IN.

www.ingramcontent.com/pod-product-compliance
Ingram Content Group UK Ltd.
Pitfield, Milton Keynes, MK11 3LW, UK
UKHW041940190726
13854UKWH00004B/1701

9 781387 311446